I Listen

and so can you.

By Dr. John G. Igwebuike

Illustrated by
Citra Lani

For permissions contact:
Dr. John G. Igwebuike
drjohnigwebuike@gmail.com
(614) 526-9872.

To my dazzling, darling daughters: Nini, Nomi, and Nata
who have taught me to L-I-S-T-E-N.

L-I-S-T-E-N

This book belongs to:

____

I listen with my right ear.

I listen with my left ear.

I listen with both of my ears.

I listen with my left, my right, and my two ears.

I listen.

I listen with my left eye.

I listen with my right eye.

I listen with both of my eyes.

I listen with my left, my right, and my two eyes.

I listen.

I listen with my look.

I listen with my lean.

I listen with my laugh.

I listen with my look, my lean, and my laugh.

I listen.

I listen with my head.

I listen with my hands.

I listen with my hug.

I listen with my head, my hands, and my hug.

I listen.

I listen with my snaps.

I listen with my claps.

I listen with my taps.

I listen with my snaps, my claps, and my taps.

I listen.

I listen with my shoes.

I listen with my moves.

I listen with my grooves.

I listen with my shoes, my moves, and my grooves.

I listen.

I listen with my hop.

I listen with my jump.

I listen with my skip.

I listen with my hop, my jump, and my skip.

I listen.

I listen with my tick.

I listen with my tock.

I listen with my time.

I listen with my tick, my tock, and my time.

I listen.

I listen with my nose.

I listen with my toes.

I listen with my rose.

I listen with my nose, my toes, and my rose.

I listen.

I listen with my mouth.

I listen with my mouth, my smile, and my grin.

I listen.

I listen with my clicks.

I listen with my clacks.

I listen with my cane.

I listen with my clicks, my clacks, and my cane.

I listen.

I listen with my arms.

I listen with my wheels.

I listen with my chair.

I listen with my arms, my wheels, and my chair.

I listen.

I listen with my Hm.

I listen with my Oh.

I listen with my Aw.

I listen with my Hm, my Oh, and my Aw.

I listen.

I listen with my cat.

I listen with my dog.

I listen with my fish.

I listen with my cat, my dog, and my fish.

I listen.

I listen with all my heart.

I listen with all my strength.

I listen with all my self.

I listen with all my heart, my strength, and my self.

I listen and so can you!

L
I
S
T
E
N

L-I-S-T-E-N

The End

www.ingramcontent.com/pod-product-compliance
Ingram Content Group UK Ltd.
Pitfield, Milton Keynes, MK11 3LW, UK
UKHW060101300726
14090UKWH00003B/342

* 9 7 8 0 9 7 1 0 0 3 7 4 3 *